Christmas

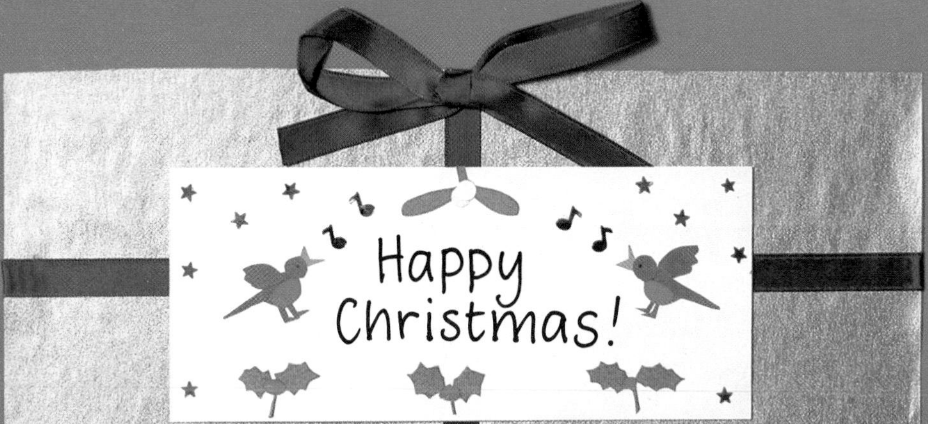

Story by Rod Theodorou
Illustrations by Annabel Collis

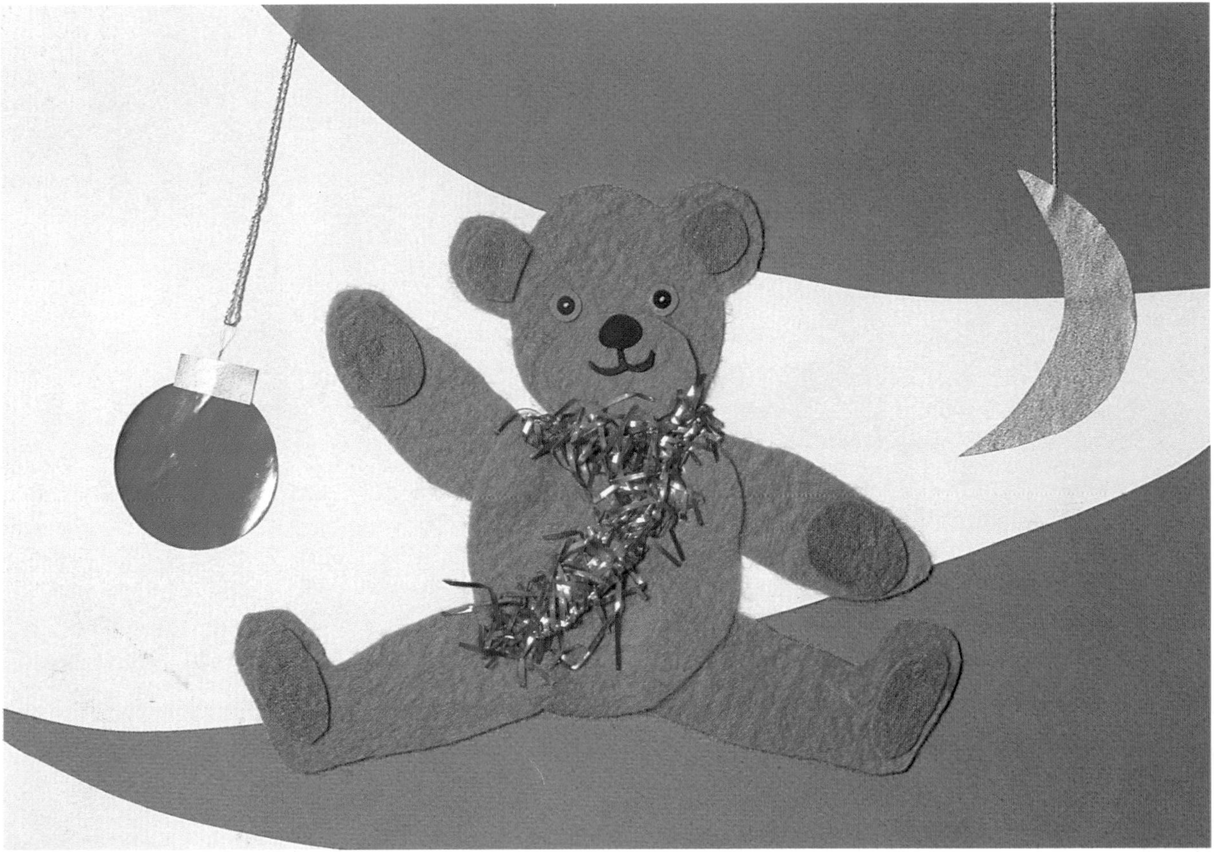

A teddy,

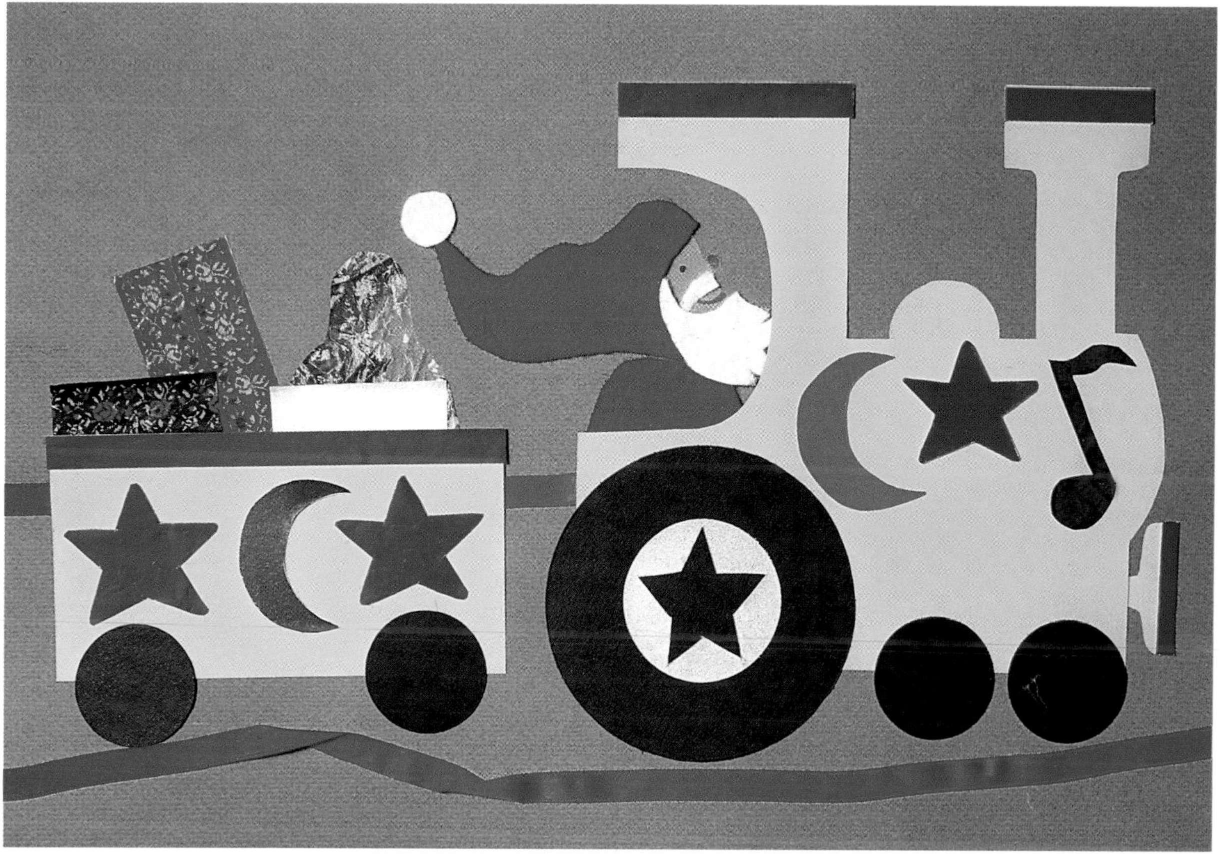

a train,

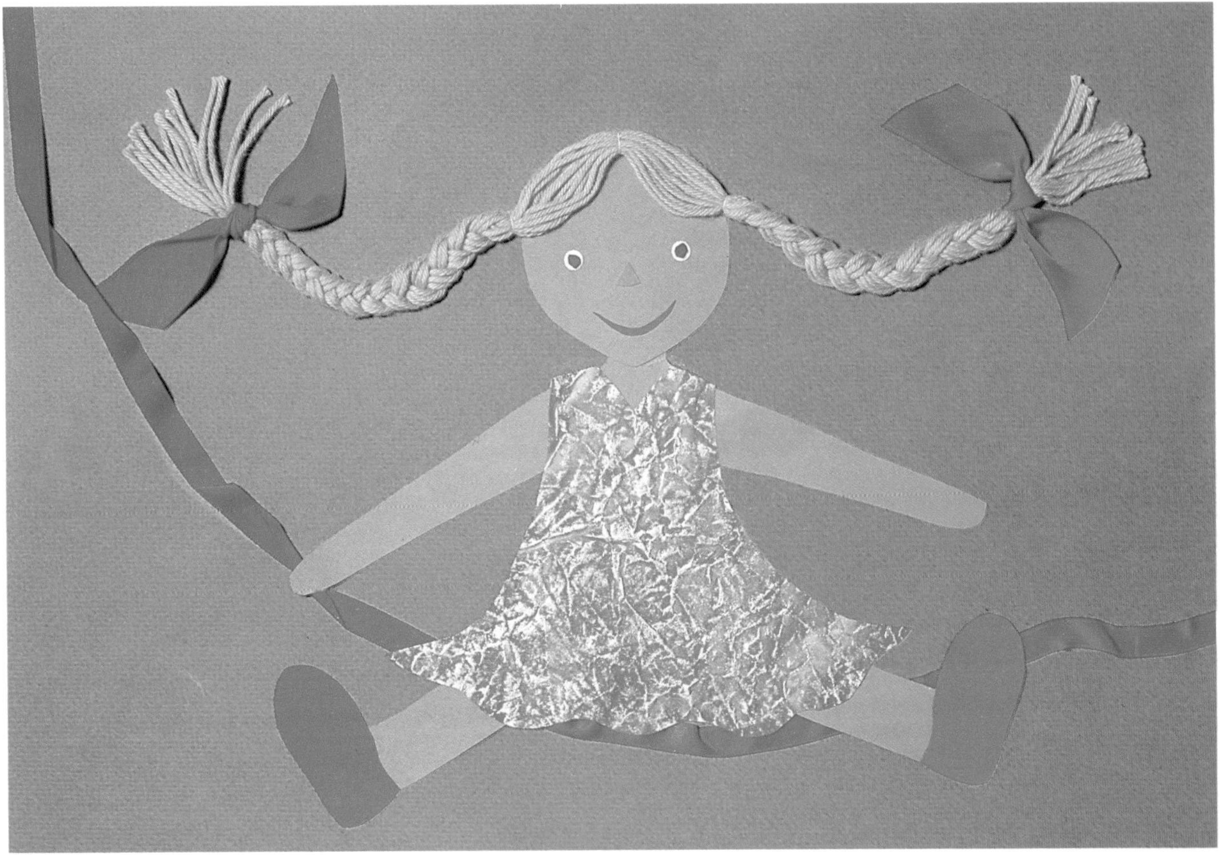

a doll,

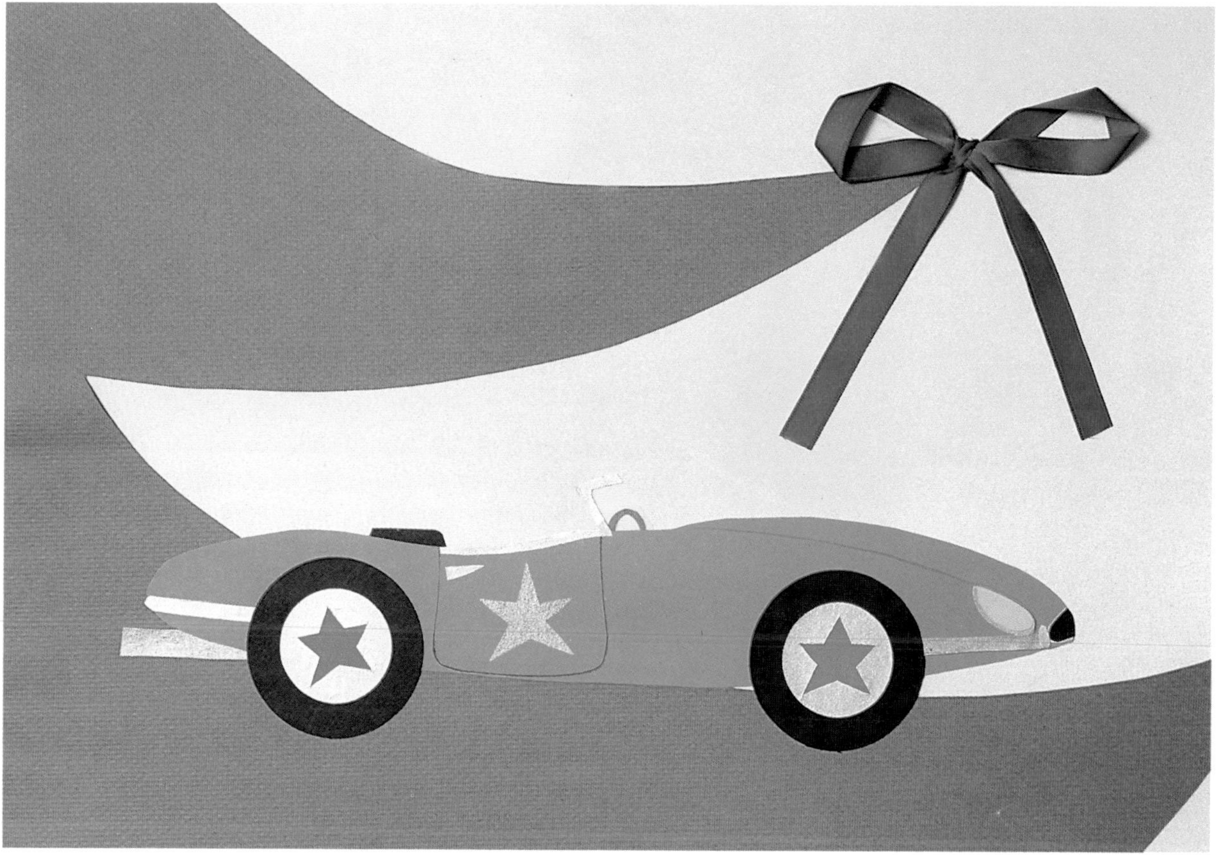

a car,

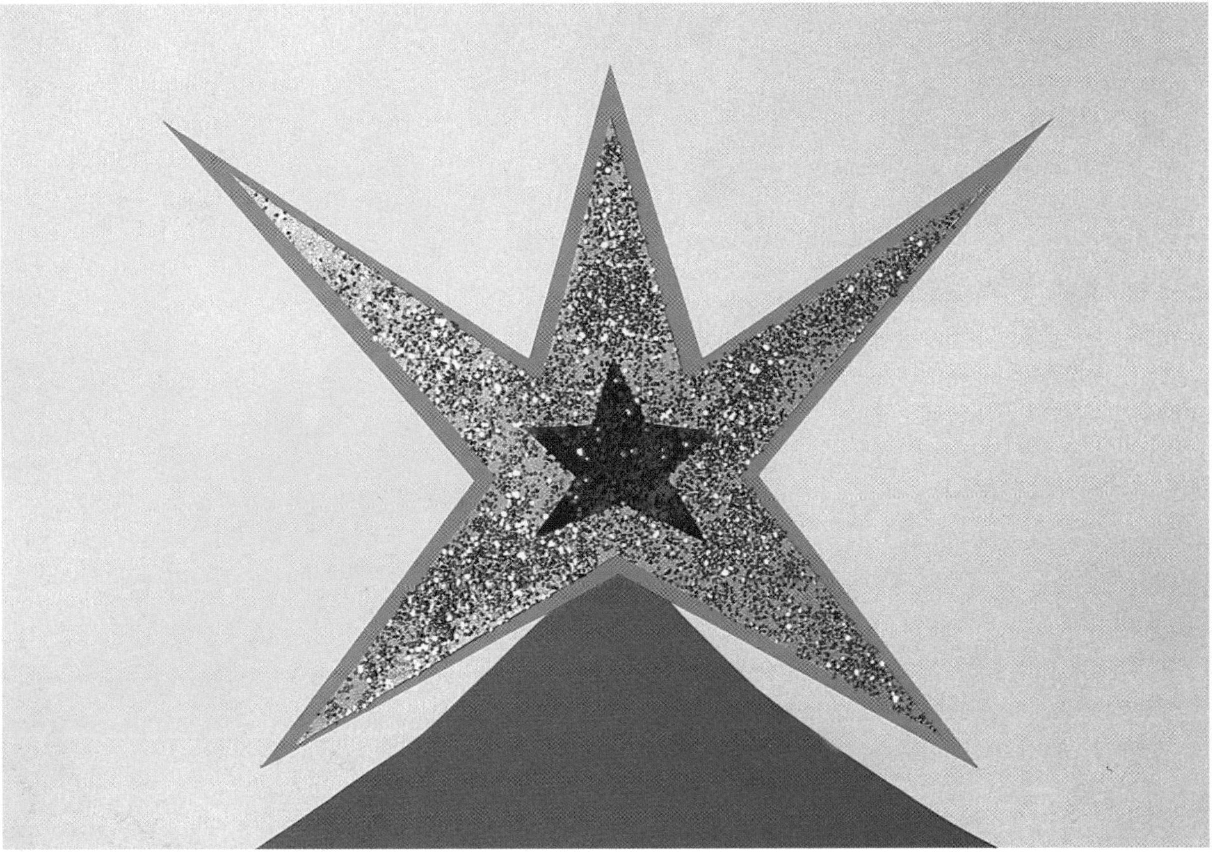

a star,

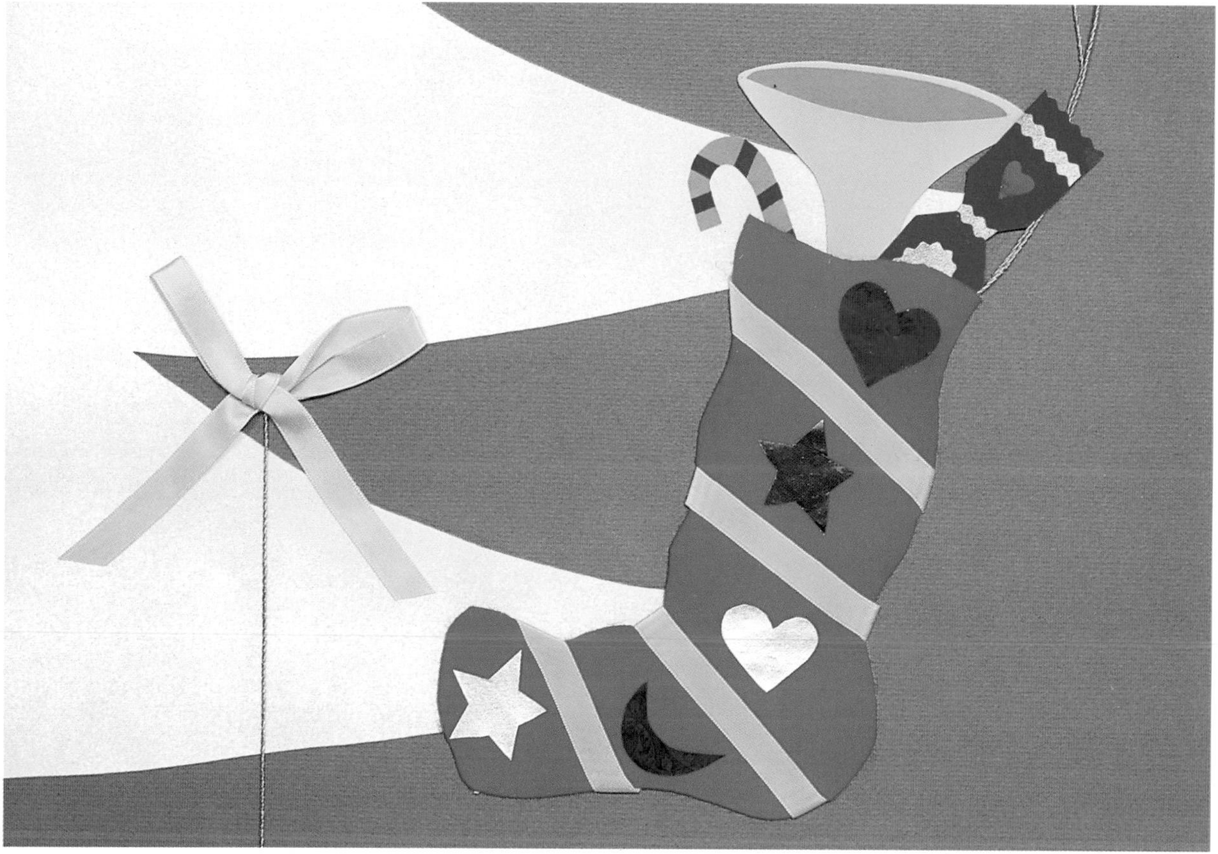

a stocking,

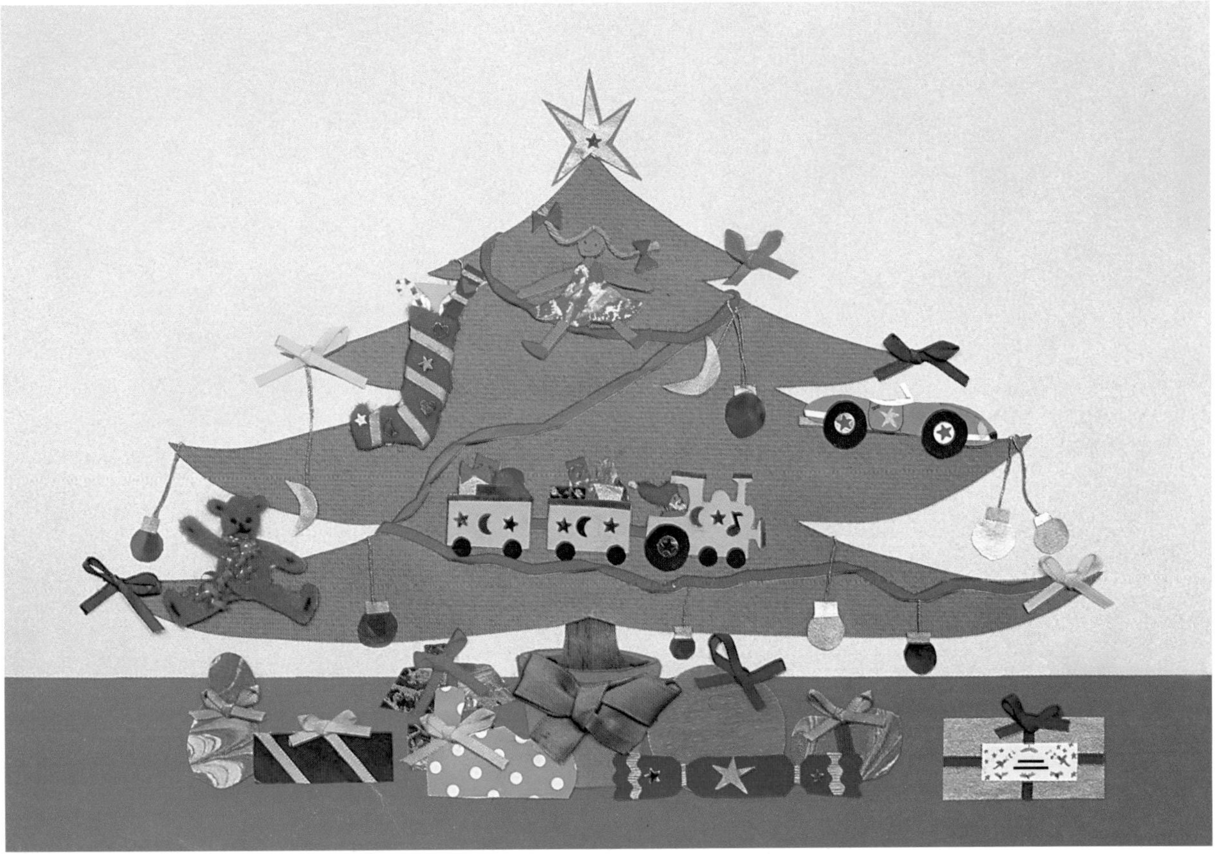

a Christmas tree!